Jil & Gail —
Sing great songs!

Sing Your Song For All You're Worth

A BOOK ON LIVING ABUNDANTLY
FOR THE YOUNG AT HEART

BY
LEO. J. FISHBECK

All rights reserved. No part of this book may be reproduced without written permission in writing from the publisher.

Copyright ©1988 by Leo Fishbeck
ISBN: 0-9619866-0-3
Printed in the United States of America

Designed by Bonita Montano

DEDICATION

This book is dedicated to Alex Vincent who sang her song for all her worth. I am tempted to say her song was all too brief, but I know it was long enough to touch the lives of untold thousands. In the final analysis, it's not how long we live, but how well we live and how much we give.

Thank you, Alex, for your gift.

ACKNOWLEDGEMENTS

My sincere gratitude to Rev. Joy Tuttle who not only encouraged me to write this book in the first place but who painstakingly transcribed the talks and performed the monumental task of the initial editing.

My thanks to Mark and Kristen for their support during the early editing stage — and to the hundreds of teenagers who taught me how to think young in the first place.

Thank you, Thalia, for your trust and support. Thank you Rod and Sandy Loomis, you know why.

And, finally, the deepest thanks of all to Raylene West. Without her encouragement, love and final editing, this book would never have gone to print.

SPECIAL GRATITUDE

A great deal of this modest work was prepared in Heavenly Manor, a cabin in Running Springs, California, appropriately named. My sincere gratitude to Marc Dumont for providing a space that made creativity easy.

TABLE OF CONTENTS

Chapter		Page
	Introduction	1
1.	Your Key To Buried Treasure	5
2.	Where Will It Come From?	9
3.	Self Worth And Courage	11
4.	How Do You *Really* Feel About Money?	15
5.	Prosperity Is Divine Love In Action	19
6.	Exercise Your Creative Imagination	23
7.	Trust In You	27
8.	Becoming More	31
9.	Healthy Desires That Help To Create Prosperity	35
10.	Negative Emotions Are O.K.	39
11.	The Laws Of Prosperity	43
12.	The Law Of Receiving Or Learning To Accept	45
13.	The Law Of Assimilation Once You Accept, It's Automatic	49
14.	The Law Of Elimination Or Making Room For The New	51
15.	The Law Of Giving Or Now That You Have It, Share It	55
16.	The Law Of Multiplication Or Why You Receive More Than You Give	59
17.	So Sing Your Song	63

Introduction

This book is based on a series of lectures that I gave to a large group of teenagers on the subject of Prosperity. Consequently, it was originally intended that this book be expressly for young people. However, many adults who have read this manuscript have strongly urged me not to limit it to any age group.

I, therefore, dedicate this book to all those who think young. That is, those who are willing to put aside old, worn out, non-productive attitudes and beliefs and examine new ideas that will enrich their lives.

I don't think that I learned to be "young at heart" until I was nearly forty years of age. As a teenager I was well on my way to becoming an old man. I didn't have anyone around to tell me about the "secrets" of prosperity when I was young, so I had to learn the hard way, through trial and error. I didn't realize then that there was a direct connection between my thoughts and my experience, and what's more, if anyone had suggested it, I would have resented it.

At the age of sixteen I came down with rheumatoid arthritis. By the time I was twenty-five, I was rapidly on my way to a wheelchair and old age. At first it was difficult for me to take responsibility for my illness. It was more comfortable to attribute it to "bad luck" or fate. But as I learned that all of my experiences were the direct result of my attitudes about life, I was able to change my ideas about myself and my world and I was healed.

Now I know whatever restriction we experience, be it physical, mental or financial, can be healed and ANYONE CAN DO IT! I trust it won't take you as long to learn this Truth as it took me. We are in a new age, an age where new ideas are coming at us at an ever increasing rate. We are beginning to see an incredible improvement of all people in the world. Our ability to grasp new concepts and exercise our imagination in constructive ways will make the difference.

A few years ago my son traveled with me on a cruise to the Mediterranean. We rode camels to the Pyramids; we visited the Holy Land and explored the ruins of the Parthenon in Athens, Greece, where Plato taught. I thought, "He's only fifteen and already experiencing the wonders of the world. I wonder where he will be going when he's my age? Probably a weekend jaunt to the moon." It took me nearly forty years to learn how to move out of a life of restriction, but only because I didn't have access to the right ideas.

A friend of mine taught a class in an elementary school. He asked sixth graders, "How many here have ever flown in an airplane?" *All* of the students raised their hands. Then he asked them where they had gone. He was barraged with the names of a variety of exotic lands. That's the age we live in. Our world is becoming smaller and the opportunities for experiencing the good life are there for anyone willing to reach out and claim them.

If you're not there yet, read on. Put into practice the techniques suggested in this book. Be patient and give yourself a chance to develop new attitudes about yourself and your world and, who knows, next year and the years to follow may find you right in the middle of experiencing your wildest dreams come true.

I can't tell you how quickly you will demonstrate your desires, but I do know that if you consistently and sincerely apply these ideas, you will experience a definite movement in the direction of realizing your dreams. To someone new and uninformed, these techniques may sound materialistic at first, a "get something for nothing" philosophy. Quite often I hear people say things like: "Learn how to pray for abundance? Aren't there more important things in life?" The answer to that lies within the Scriptures themselves, which clearly state that there is a direct tie between Spirituality and abundance. Somewhere along the line, somebody got the idea that it was more blessed to be poor. This is a misunderstanding of the Scriptures.

Actually, prosperity is a demonstration of a certain level of Spirituality, provided we correctly define the word "prosperity." I know a lot of very wealthy people who, with all of their money, are still empty, unhappy, lonely and desperate. I know of one person who was spending $1,000 a week on cocaine. That's a lot of money *and* a lot of unhappiness. It's certainly not my definition of prosperity.

True prosperity should be defined as having the freedom to do what you want to do when you want to do it, provided that it is for your highest good and in the best interests of all concerned. In short, the abundant life lets you be the very best person you can possibly be. Isn't it better to give *that* to the world rather than a depressed, negative and pessimistic outlook on life?

If you *are* young, reading this book may prevent you from

falling into the pits, or belief systems that have caused the older generation so many problems. Whatever your age, if you are young at heart, meaning that your curiosity about life and the enthusiasm for new ideas have not been squelched, you may very well find within these pages an opportunity to move into an entirely new level of abundant living.

You have every right to an abundant life. You have every right to enjoy that life. Claim your right to a life of prosperity and happiness now by deciding to establish new attitudes and beliefs about yourself and your world. Begin NOW . . . this very moment to accept and believe: "I am open and receptive to the Infinite Good that comes to me by right of my new beliefs about prosperity. I take great delight in knowing that I AM WORTHY OF THE ABUNDANT LIFE."

Chapter 1

Your Key To Buried Treasure

*"A few can touch the magic string
and noisy fame is proud to win them.*

*Alas, for those that never sing,
but die with all their music in them."*

Oliver Wendell Holmes

There's no such thing as being stuck in a present condition. That is a Spiritual impossibility. There are definite techniques which will enable you to move from where you are to where you want to be. By changing your thoughts and your feelings, you can change your experiences. Many people appear to be dependent on others for their income, i.e., young people, housewives, invalids and retired people. They might say, "How can I demonstrate abundance in my life through a change in my thinking when I'm not working and I rely totally on others for an income? Shouldn't I pray that they give me more money?" All I can say is that your prosperity has nothing to do with what anyone else will do for you. I have known many people who, once they have altered their belief system, have demonstrated an increased level of income from an entirely unexpected source.

You see, there's a Law of Mind that responds to your faith and belief. It is the one thing we can't get away from so we might as well understand It and use It constructively. Whatever your current condition is in terms of your prosperity, it is a direct result of your thinking at the conscious and unconscious levels. That's the part that hurts, but unless we accept it, how in the world are we ever going to take the initiative and change? As long as we think someone has to do it for us we are powerless because we cannot change or control other people.

We are all living in a Universe of abundance. God has seen to that. But you and I are responsible for extracting our share from this abundant Universe. If abundance is everywhere then we need to figure out how to relate to the Universe in such a way that we can become a channel through which we receive our portion. The way to do this is to work solely with ourselves because we really can't work in any other way. We don't have to convince God because God's work is already done and it certainly doesn't do any good to try to manipulate others.

You can reach a point where prosperity just happens effortlessly to you. You might say, "Do I have to go to work?" I don't know. Most well meaning people will advise you to go to work. Personally, I believe there is only one reason to work and that is to submit to a deep seated need to express yourself which is vital to your sense of well-being. "Work is love made visible," according to Kahlil Gibran. It's important to work, but if you say "I *HAVE* to work in order to make money," the Law of Mind says, "Amen brother . . . So be it!"

A friend of mine, a millionaire, had two sons who were very involved in automobile racing. They had a unique financial agreement with their dad. One of his sons came to him one day and said, "Dad, I want to buy a new sports car." His father said, "All right, you know the deal. You come up with half of the money and I'll contribute the other half." The son gave a big sigh of resignation and said, "I guess that means I'll have to go to work." His father replied, "Well son, if that's your consciousness."

In other words, that *might* be the way, but as far as Infinite Mind is concerned, there are limitless ways in which you can experience prosperity. The boys' father worked only a couple of days each month. The rest of the time he devoted his creative abilities towards charitable efforts. He just gave his time away and he did it out of love. He knew he had to "work" because it was a necessary part of his expression of life, but he didn't have to work in order to make money.

It's important to be clear on this. Work? Yes ... if you want to experience a meaningful, creative, active life. But if you want to experience a prosperous life as well, put into practice the techniques that follow. They can help you attract an entirely new level of prosperity into your life and give you the freedom to express life in a far more fulfilling way.

Your prosperity already exists. It's like buried treasure. You may not yet be enjoying it, but it is most assuredly there, waiting to be discovered, waiting to be uncovered. ONLY YOU HAVE THE KEY!

Chapter 2

Where Will It Come From?

If everything comes from God and if God is everywhere present, there can't be anything outside of God, which means we are all immersed in the gifts of Spirit. The total goodness of God must be available to everyone. Now, can you conceive of this loving Father, this giving Presence saying, "You, over there, are going to receive a little bit more because you're so-so, and you there, I'm going to give you an unlimited supply because you're great?" Can you imagine an Infinite Intelligence doing this? If you can't, and if you do believe that God gives to all unconditionally, then why don't we all receive the bounty of life equally? If it isn't Infinite Mind that determines how much you shall receive, then it must be you, or should I say, what you are doing with your individualized use of Infinite Mind.

A sixty year old woman whom I was counseling said to me one day, "My husband is retiring and we don't have enough money to keep up the payments on our house." She tried to convince me to pray for her husband so that he would make enough money that they might continue to live in their beautiful home. I told her, "It doesn't work that way. If you pray for him to make money and you don't change your own belief system, he may make more money allright, but he also might end up spending it on another woman who has a belief system for attracting wealthy men." That got her attention. She became quite indignant and said, "Well, what do you expect me to do? Do you think the money is going to come falling down out of the sky?" "Well," I said, "I suppose it could happen that way, but it doesn't have to." She rather begrudgingly agreed to work on her own beliefs concerning the source of money.

The following week at our next appointment, the first words out of her mouth were, "You and your damned prayers!" "What's the matter?" I asked. She replied with a tone of voice that expressed disgust, humor and excitement, "I have a job!" She had never worked a day in her life and yet an opportunity literally fell into her lap that was just perfect for her. She became a salesperson for a jewelry company. She had a gift of gab that wouldn't quit and a natural talent for sales work. She not only made money but she filled her jewelry box to overflowing. What's more, she was actively and creatively involved with people and life.

Stretch your mind. Don't get caught up in the prison of thinking that your prosperity must come from one particular source. In his book, "The Science of Mind," Ernest Holmes says, "There is only one way that God can give to us and that is through us." What does that mean, *"through us?"* Read on!

Chapter 3

Self Worth And Courage

Two ingredients necessary to establish a prosperity consciousness are SELF WORTH and COURAGE.

First and foremost is *SELF WORTH.* If you are the channel through which the gifts of Spirit are expressed in your outer life, how can Infinite Mind give through an individual whose thinking will not permit it to happen?

This givingness is the result of the unconditional Love of God. The gifts of Spirit are free. Everything is bestowed upon us out of the Love of God. If we do not greet these gifts in an attitude of self love then it means we are greeting them in an attitude of self hate. It's either one or the other. If you are resenting yourself, then you are restricting this flow of good. You can't resent yourself and love God at the same time, It's a mental impossibility. So, if you resent yourself, you are also resenting God because you are a living expression of God. How in the world can Infinite Mind go against It's own Nature and express through an outlet that cannot respond to It? It cannot demand that you be receptive any more than water can increase its rate of flow by creating a larger diameter pipe.

You literally put the brakes on yourself and your good when

you do not feel worthy. WORTHY! Self Worth means, "I am somebody!" That "somebody" is not the conditioned you, it's not the limited you, it's not the you that is caught up in your feelings of inferiority or your feelings of condemnation. That "somebody" is the REAL YOU, the beautiful expression of God that you are in Truth. That "somebody" IS the gift of Spirit, and word of God that you are right now!

You are that special person, but it won't do you a bit of good until you agree to it. It isn't a simple job. If you have already spent a number of years convincing yourself that you are not worthy, it may take a little time for you to rework your consciousness into one of absolute and unconditional self love.

The second essential attitude to embody is COURAGE. Once you begin to dedicate yourself to the realization that you are worthy, you must then have the courage to act from the new self. That means the kind of courage it takes to stand before a mirror and say, "I love you." That's hard for some people to do. It means the courage to accept gifts from those around you as gifts of love, whatever form they may take. Accept them in a consciousness of self worth, not out of guilt, but out of a quiet realization that says, "I deserve this gift and I'm glad that this person sees something worthwhile in me."

It means the *COURAGE* to stick your neck out occasionally; the willingness to fail or to be rejected when you stand for something you believe in. It means pursuing a path that sometimes does not meet with the approval of those close to you. Demonstrating that kind of courage can be a major step towards personal success.

As you get in touch with your own unique nature you will be moving into unexplored territory. That can be scary. Life is full of wrong turns, dead ends, mistakes and people rejecting us. If you try to live your life free of such experiences, it means you will be standing still, making no choices and getting nowhere at all.

No, there's no need to avoid such events when you know that you have a limitless inner reserve of energy, creative imagination and determination that will enable you to meet them head on. The inevitable result is that you will become stronger, and strength leads to success.

Such courage is possible when you are aware of your inner resources. Believe in yourself and know that you possess, as a Divine Inheritance, infinite wisdom and limitless energy. Learn to tap into that ultimate Reality of your Being. When you are aware of your inner capabilities, it is much easier to deal with criticism, failure and disappointments, because they do not become your gods. The less power you give them, the more power you have to grow through such experiences. In retrospect, you will discover that they, in fact, gave you a stronger foundation for living a successful and prosperous life, because you had the courage to stick your neck out and SING *YOUR* SONG.

Chapter 4

How Do You *Really* Feel About Money?

There is a Scriptural validation related to the idea of prosperity that needs to be clearly understood. A careful study of the Bible, particularly the Old Testament, reveals that the people who were considered to be the most Spiritual, those who were the great contributors to enlightened thinking, the most highly regarded, were usually very wealthy people — millionaires by our standards. As we read about their many accomplishments we find that, usually, the account ends with the statement, "And he was favored by God." According to the ancient authors of the Scriptures, there must be a connection between prosperity and Spirituality.

Why would these leaders of the past even teach the law of tithing 3,000 years ago unless the purpose of their teaching was to validate the fact that it was right and acceptable for them to experience abundance? When you read the Scriptures in this light you will find statement after statement referring to the idea of abundance as a part of God's blessing.

Let's try a little exercise in imagery. Sometimes the active use of imagination can help you get in touch with your true feelings. With your eyes closed and resting in a relaxed position, have someone read the following statements to you. Ask them to read slowly, pausing after each statement. If no one is available at the moment, you may read the statements to yourself. Be sure to retain the image you have and to be very aware of the feelings you are experiencing as you read each statement.

> *Visualize that you have in front of you a wallet or a purse. Inside the wallet or purse is a five dollar bill. Imagine taking the five dollar bill out of the wallet or purse and spreading it out in front of you. Take a good look at it. President Lincoln is on the front of it. Continue to get a good, clear picture of the bill in your mind. What does it look like? What condition is it in? When you have a good picture of the bill and what it looks like, put the bill into your mouth. (Remember, it's an imaginary bill.) Now that the bill is in your mouth, begin to chew it. Don't swallow it. Keep chewing it. Just chew and chew and chew. Be aware of what you are experiencing. What are your sensations? (If you are reading this, close your eyes and continue to chew the bill for two or three moments until it is good and soggy.) Now, check your feelings. Take the bill out of your mouth and review the feelings you had. Did it taste strange or bad? What did the bill look like before you put it into your mouth? Was it crumpled up and old? Was it torn or defaced? Did you have trouble putting it into your mouth? If so, why? Did it seem dirty to you?*

Here's the point. *You* had absolute freedom to create the bill. *You* determined what it looked like. You created that bill out of your own mind and consciousness. If you created a bill that was wrinkled or torn or dirty, then you need to ask yourself, "Why? Why would I, having absolute freedom to imagine any kind of bill I wanted to, create that?" If you had a problem putting the bill into your mouth because you saw it as dirty, remember, you could have imagined it as being brand new and right out of the mint, all fresh and clean. You had the freedom of choice, so you need to look at why you chose to create the bill as you did. The experience was entirely YOURS.

It is just possible that this exercise will give you a little hint as to what your attitude about money really is. Think about it. When we put anything into our mouths it is a very intimate experience. We only put into our mouths that which we feel safe and comfortable with. It's a very personal experience.

Perhaps you now have an idea of what you need to do in terms of changing your attitude about money. It can be an important step in the development of your consciousness.

Chapter 5

Prosperity Is Divine Love In Action

If there is a direct relationship between feelings of worthiness and the prosperous life, one of the most important gifts you can give yourself is self love.

The Spiritual basis for self love is that there is a Power which is the Presence of God within you and It is now affirming about you, as It said to Jesus of Nazareth, "This is my beloved in whom I am well pleased." ... Math. 3:17. If you can agree with that statement and respond to it by entering into a commitment that likewise affirms, "*I* am the beloved in whom I am well pleased," you will have made the necessary connection, the discovery of true self love. If God loves you and you love you, there is no power on earth that can limit or restrict you.

You are responsible for your prosperity. You are responsible for your life. It isn't enough that God loves you. It isn't enough that Infinite Mind finds great joy in expressing It's bountiful good in your life. Without your cooperation and acceptance, all of this good will pass you by.

It's like holding a cup under the waterfall upside down. The water is there in unlimited amounts — the force of it, the goodness of it — but you're not getting any. It's up to you to turn the cup right side up and receive the good that is already available to you. The only way you can do this, the only way you can provide a mold that will permit prosperity to move into your life, is through your acknowledgment that you are a loving expression of Divine Mind, the Source of all good, and then follow that acknowledgment with the conscious act of loving and accepting yourself unconditionally.

There's a reason why there's so much talk about accepting and loving the self, because when you are experiencing the prosperous life it means that you are also INTO a life of love. When you have reached the point where you can accept the beautiful, abundant Nature that you are, when you can truly believe that you are a beautiful gift of Spirit, then you are IN love, not with any thing or anyone special. You are just IN LOVE.

Love is a verb, not a noun. We really can't give each other love. I can experience love as it moves through you to me but only if I have first learned to accept and love myself. You can't give love to me, because you are not the source. But I can sure enjoy your being the channel for my loving experience, once I qualify for it by setting myself straight. It isn't enough to simply know we have God's Love. We have a legitimate need to experience that Love through the people in our world. You have every right to affirm, "God loves me by means of people." We all have a valid need to experience love from others. It will happen easily and spontaneously when we get the sequence straight. First, accept God's love of you. Second, love yourself unconditionally. Third, let yourself love and care for others, and finally let the love of others enter into your life.

Implied in this sequence is an all important factor: You cannot truly experience love while at the same time holding resentment towards anyone. If you are holding a grudge, you are withholding the gifts of Spirit and preventing them from expressing in your life. If you think that you may be harboring resentment towards anyone, work immediately on releasing it. You simply can't afford it.

You experience love in a very tangible way when you discover that you have the ability to be IN love. As you learn to love and accept yourself and everyone in your world unconditionally, you automatically establish a basis by which prosperity can move effortlessly into your experience. This happens when, both consciously and subconsciously, you are affirming, "I am a beloved expression of God. I am worthy of the good life and I claim it now as my Divine Inheritance."

As a result of your ability to be IN love, you assume your Spiritual responsibility by becoming an open channel through which the good life flows into and manifests in your world. It is in this way that Infinite Mind expresses as prosperity in your life.

Chapter 6

Exercise Your Creative Imagination

The next step towards an expanded prosperity consciousness is to develop your CREATIVE IMAGINATION. The most unhappy people I know are the ones who lose sight of their ability to exercise their imagination in positive ways. Their vision of their future becomes limited, because they can't see their way out of certain situations. They live in the illusion that there's no way out, therefore never availing themselves of the opportunity of getting in touch with the wonderful potential that is within them.

Whenever you encounter an obstacle and you work your way through it successfully, you are exercising your creative imagination. A creative mind never accepts dead ends but considers all problems as puzzles to be solved. The creative mind sees beyond the effect to the limitless possibilities of positive action. The more able you are to see life from different points of view, the less likely you will be fooled by temporary setbacks. There are many good ways to approach any problem. All that you need is one of them!

You exercise your creative imagination by refusing to accept verdicts. Only the ego in people says, "It can't be done." There is no problem created by the mind of man that is greater than Infinite Intelligence. You are one with that Intelligence and therefore you have the potential ability to see clearly the perfect way to resolve any dilemma, be it in career, relationships or prosperity.

Get used to practicing seeing situations from more than one point of view. De-hypnotize yourself. Let go of your ego and approach each obstacle with the conviction, "There's always a way." The more you broaden your perspective, the easier it will be to exercise your creative imagination and discover new ways to live life more effectively.

When I teach my Prosperity Course, I always give my students an assignment at the first class. They must create something that they have never done before and bring it in for the rest of the students to see at the last class. Some find this very stressful because they feel limited in their creative ability and are afraid to show others what they might consider to be an "inferior" effort.

This resistance may be the very reason why they are not demonstrating prosperity in their lives. It's vitally important for you to stretch your creative muscles and see yourself and your capabilities in a larger way.

Be willing to have your initial effort be less than perfect. I tell my students that I don't expect them to be a Walt Whitman or a Rembrandt — nor does anyone else. The point is that they have the courage to try and exercise new dimensions of their creative ability. How many creative projects never get off the ground because of the fear of failure or rejection? What fun everyone has at the conclusion of the last class sharing the results of their new creative efforts. It is always a fantastic arts and crafts show and a justifiable cause for celebration.

I urge you to try it. Select something that you've never done before and spend three to four weeks on it. If it's stressful, so much the better. Remember, don't worry about the quality of the completed effort. That's not the point. The point is that you had the courage to experiment with a new dimension of your creative potential. Oh, yes, when you've completed it, muster up the courage to show it to your friends. Overcome your fear of criticism and get used to showing the world your best effort today knowing that tomorrow it will be better IF YOU STAY WITH IT! Go ahead and do it. I dare you! It could be the most important step you will ever take towards a more prosperous life.

Chapter 7

Trust In You

Many years ago I had a Spiritual experience. It occurred at a time when I was very troubled over a decision I had made. I had serious doubts as to whether or not I was doing the right thing because I felt as though, as a result, I might incur a considerable amount of disfavor and lose certain friends. It had taken courage to act on my decision and I couldn't help feeling guilty, wondering, "Am I doing the right thing?"

I was in the process of taking some out-of-town visitors on a tour of Forest Lawn, a world famous cemetery where many outstanding works of art are displayed. We had just finished viewing the famous stained glass window, "The Last Supper." As we left the viewing room, we walked down a long corridor. Marble crypts were on either side where bodies were buried. The group had gone on ahead of me. For some reason I lagged behind. I wasn't thinking about anything in particular. I wasn't even thinking about my problem.

Suddenly, I was struck by a strong realization. It demanded my attention. These experiences never have words, so all I can do is share with you roughly the idea that moved through me. It said, "Look at the crypts on either side of you and know this: 95% of the people represented in those crypts never had the courage to do what you are doing." I was healed. This sudden realization washed away all of my anxiety and concern. A great burden was lifted from me. I realized that I had acted out of an intuitive guidance and courage when I had made my decision.

It also said this: "On the day you die, you will bless the fact that you had the courage to act." I know now that this is true because today, sixteen years later, I'm still being blessed by that decision.

I share this story because it was an experience that changed my life. I realized, in that moment, that there are far too many people who have a song inside of them, but don't trust their ability to sing it.

We're too caught up in going where the "buck" is. We're too concerned with getting the job that will win the approval of others. We forget that God gave us a gift, a song to sing and if we don't sing it, how can the world applaud us? Life has no meaning if we don't feel that we are contributing to it. Trust your interests, your desires, what you enjoy doing. Let them inspire you into action. Put some sincere effort into them. Where would great singers be if they never took the time to practice?

How will you know when you begin to sing your song? God has a way of letting you know. It's called joy. You will have great fun in doing it. You will have a sense of pride and accomplishment as you enjoy the finished product. You will have a sense of purpose, and finally you will receive admiration and appreciation from those who are benefited by your gift.

No matter what you have thought about yourself in the past, it's time to stop judging and start trusting. It's time to realize that you deserve the "good life." The "good life" is a life of love. It is a life of prosperity and a life of giving of yourself in ways that bless you and enrich everyone around you. You are already a gift, but a gift is only a gift when it is given. Trust in your ability to discover yours.

You can do it when you believe that Infinite Mind never made a mistake. Life knew just what It was doing when It chose to express the magnificent personage and individuality that you are.

Chapter 8

Becoming More

This is not intended to be a "get-something-for-nothing" scheme. Too many people have used metaphysical principles in an attempt to heal effects. They say, "Pray for health and you get health; pray for money and you get money." It's not that simple. Dr. Ernest Holmes, in his book, "The Science of Mind," clearly states, "IF YOU WANT TO EXPERIENCE MORE, YOU MUST BECOME MORE." Prayer really does work. But if you pray for something and do not support the prayer with the proper mental attitudes, then what is the Law of Mind going to do?

For example, let's say you need money and you spend fifteen minutes a day praying for it. Then the rest of the day you complain about what you don't have. When you look at the clothes in your closet and are unhappy with them or when you look at your car and see all the things that need to be repaired, or in one way or another condemn that which you already possess, you are in effect, cursing your present circumstance. This only serves to reinforce the problem. You are placing in mind a belief that "What I now have is bad." The more you support that negative belief, the more the Law of Mind will tend to produce that experience into your life. Being upset with what you have or don't have does not support affirmative prayer.

Now, what's the difference between a prayer and an attitude? Actually, most attitudes have more power than a prayer. What you believe most of the day is likely to have more power than what you try to believe for fifteen minutes a day. Your reactions to life are indicators of a belief system that is already within the subconscious. It is thinking its way up into your conscious awareness and comes out as a reaction.

When you react negatively, you are dealing with a fundamental belief. So if you are worried, concerned or upset about what you don't have, that is a basic reaction to your world of effects born out of a deep-seated belief that you are not abundant. THIS is the attitude that the Law of Mind responds to and consequently, tends to produce more of the same.

How can we expect to overcome a whole day of reactions and negative attitudes with just fifteen minutes of Prayer? The Law of Mind doesn't know the difference between a prayer, an attitude or a reaction.

If you want to experience more, you must become more. You must learn to live your life as though you really believed in your prayers. This does not mean looking at your circumstance through rose-colored glasses, nor does it suggest that you should lie to yourself or ignore the problem. It does mean that you must live your life in the realization that whatever it is you desire already exists at some point in mind as a fundamental reality, and that you must let your conscious mind function out of that Truth because the Truth is that God has already provided you with a life of Prosperity. If you will let your day-to-day attitudes reflect that reality, you will be providing the means by which that which you seek will move into your outer experience where you may enjoy it.

There is no need to pretend that you don't have the problem. Your subconscious is not likely to buy it anyway. Pretending comes across as lying. Besides, if you were really convinced, there wouldn't be any need to pray in the first place. In your attempt to change your present condition, it is important that you view it realistically. It may be a fact that you have a financial problem, in which case it is appropriate to say, "Yes, that's right. I don't have enough money to buy what I want." For the moment, that may be a fact of life. What you want is not currently in your experience. Your awareness of lack and wanting more is a healthy desire! Desire is the starting point for creating new conditions.

As you begin to work with your new attitude, that is, thinking out of the Divine Reality, don't be surprised if you hear yourself arguing. We all have a "yeah but" inside of us that we have to deal with from time to time. If you try to rise above your negative feelings and say, "I am perfect love," your "yeah but" may say, "Yeah, but I'm still feeling rejected." If you say, "I am abundant," it may respond with, "Yeah, but I can't pay the bills." When this happens you don't go to war with "Yeah but." You don't need to fight your doubts. You simply understand that the source of their information is nothing but deep-seated false beliefs. By realizing this you are more able to pray in Truth and keep your thoughts aligned with Divine realities.

How do we pray in TRUTH? We pray in Truth by recognizing that beyond our experience, there is a Spiritual Truth, an Original Truth that you and I were born with and even though we are not experiencing that Truth in this moment, by aligning ourselves with It, It will manifest in our lives.

When we pray for money, let's realize that we must support that prayer with an attitude and a fundamental belief system that says, "In spite of my experience, I am one with the abundant Universe." That means that you are no longer seduced by your experience, that you are not allowing the effect to run your thinking processes and that you can begin to live in a certain aura of confidence.

Do your best to think and pray out of the realization that you already are where you want to be. Rather than beg God for more money, lift yourself to the awareness that Today you can live in the consciousness of God's supply and assume your Divine Inheritance. Remember, if you wish to experience more, you must become more.

Chapter 9

Healthy Desires That Help To Create Prosperity

There are two desires that appear to be very important for a prosperity consciousness. One is the desire to travel and the other is the desire to improve your environment. If you pay attention to these two desires and make a sincere effort to satisfy them, you will forever be experiencing newness and beauty in your life. You will travel all over the world and wherever you are, you will be striving to make the world you live in more beautiful.

People who lose their desire to experience more of their world and who don't care about improving the conditions they live in, are stagnant. They are living in a poverty consciousness regardless of how much money they have.

Many years ago, I was driving to my office one day and complaining to myself because I had not yet fulfilled one of my fondest desires, to travel and see the world. I had been raised in rural upstate New York and had never been beyond a hundred miles from home. I was fourteen years old before I crossed the state border. Although I really loved to travel, it just didn't appear possible to fulfill my desire. So, there I was complaining, "I can't go anywhere. Oh, how I'd love to see all of the wonderful, exotic places I've heard so much about." I felt very limited and restricted.

Suddenly an idea moved through me . . . an awakening. It said, "You're already there. You already have the ability to travel anywhere you want to go in this world." The idea made so much sense to me that I can remember breathing a sigh of relief as I actually felt the reality of this Truth.

This deep feeling of "knowing" came as a result of doing my homework. You see, it doesn't happen to us out of the blue. It happens when we keep knowing the Truth. It happens when we keep working with the idea of Reality until, eventually, something within the subconscious says, "Yes, that's really true." It is then that we begin to experience it in our outer world.

I realized I could combine my need to teach and inspire and my desire to travel by taking groups of people on seminars throughout the world. A few weeks later I was making plans to take my first trip to Hawaii. Since then, I have cruised the Carribean Sea, the Mediterranean Sea and the inland passage to Alaska. I have visited Spain, Sicily, North Africa, the South Seas, Fiji, Tahiti and Samoa. I have explored the great Pyramids of Giza, the Holy Land, the ruins of Athens, the Greek Islands, Turkey, Japan, Hong Kong, Singapore, Bangkok, People's Republic of China, Russia, the Scandanavian Capitals and I know there are many more adventures to come. The point I am making is that it was so incredibly easy once the full realization of the Truth finally hit home.

Why is the desire for travel a healthy sign? Because when you want to experience more of your world it means you are stretching your awareness beyond your present environment. When you satisfy your curiosity to know more about the rest of your world, you are responding to a deep urge to expand your horizons. You become more aware of the part you play in the whole.

I'm not saying you can do it easily. I am saying that every thought of Truth you entertain will tend to accumulate and become a part of your belief system. I do know that every thought of Truth you consider has greater power than your limited thinking. Why? Because when you are reacting to your so called limitations, when you are griping about them or worried about them, there is no basic law or principle in the Universe that supports those ideas of limitation. In other words, there isn't some kind of principle of lack floating around which suddenly descends on you saying, "I am a principle of lack. Zap! Now you are limited." There is nothing to support your feelings of restriction except YOUR OWN BELIEF SYSTEM.

On the other hand, every time you utter a statement of Truth relating to the idea that "I am one with the abundant Universe," you have the full agreement of God. The entire Universe supports every statement of Truth that you make. That's why it doesn't take us as long to get out of a problem as it did to get into it. When you make a statement of Truth, the basic impulse of the entire Creative Universe is behind you. That is why if you keep at it, if you are persistent, IT WORKS!

There's nothing wrong with wanting good things. There's nothing wrong with wanting to travel or to surround yourself with beauty. When you want to beautify where you live, it means that you are aligned with one of the most important of all Spiritual Laws, the Law of Evolution. That is to say, there is something about life that always wants to improve on itself.

Life continues to unfold and get better. By satisfying your healthy desire to surround yourself with that which you deem beautiful, you are fully participating in this vital principle of

Life. It means you are identifying with your own inner beauty which, since it's a part of this same law, continues to become more beautiful. In fact, your desire to establish more beauty in your environment is your own evolving inner beauty urging itself into outer expression. It suggests to you that whatever beauty you may be enjoying today, there is something even more beautiful to behold tomorrow.

God gave you the ability to enjoy your world. Can you imagine a capricious God that would say, "I'll give you the ability to enjoy the good things in life but you can't have them"? That doesn't make sense, does it? If you have the ability to enjoy the good in life, it's because there is something within you that deserves it. As far as Infinite Mind is concerned, the fact that you deserve it is already established. Now all you have to do is agree with it.

Chapter 10

Negative Emotions Are O.K.

Positive and negative emotions are likely to be with us throughout our lives. I have already indicated that. If you are praying to know that you are worthy of an abundant life, feelings of unworthiness may deny your prayers. The Law of Mind responds to your reaction of self hate. It doesn't know that you may be just reacting to a momentary occurrence. As far as it is concerned, you are giving validity to a belief system and reinforcing it. That is why it is so important to love yourself.

I want to make one point very clear and this is important. I don't mean to imply that when you have these negative reactions you should think, "Oh, now I'm not being a good person." If you feel guilty about your negative thoughts, you add to the problem. It's O.K. to be honest when you experience a negative emotion. It's O.K. to validate the fact that you're hurting. That may be an important step in your healing. Yes, your negative reactions can be your teacher, if you learn to handle them properly.

All your feelings are important and should not be invalidated. A feeling of pain is a signal that you are ready to grow. When you are feeling the hurt of limitation, why are you feeling it? Because the Law of Life is saying to you, "It's time to move up and out of your present experience and enter a new level of fulfillment." The pain, anxiety and the fears regarding money are nothing more than life readying you for that all important next step in realizing your potential freedom. We can become alert to that next step through pain.

In Athens, Greece, up above the city, are the famous ruins of the Acropolis and the great Parthenon where Plato taught. At the very top of the hill is a smaller structure called "The Temple of the Wingless Victory." At one time it contained a famous statue of a woman with shorn wings. The reason she was called "Wingless Victory" was to illustrate the vital principle that the only true victory you can experience is when you don't fly away from your problems.

We can use Metaphysics to run away from a problem and ignore the fact that we are still operating out of a belief system that is in opposition to our affirmations. We can hide the pain and say, "God is good" ... "God is everywhere" ... "I am one with God," etc., and completely ignore and cover up our pain because we think we are not supposed to feel it.

Have you ever had hunger pains? Normally, as long as you know there is food available, your response to that pain is, "So, I'm hungry but I'm going to have lunch soon so I'll be O.K." It isn't the hunger pain that's upsetting you. You can handle that pain, can't you? This "hunger pang" keeps you alive. Those who lose it, die. If you lose your appetite you don't eat and when you don't eat, the body disintegrates. When you know the food will be there, you can cope with the pain. It's only when you fear that there is no food available that the strong negative panic reactions set in.

The pain is a signal that it's time to experience fulfillment. That's all it is and that's all it was ever intended to be. I don't care if it's a physical pain, an emotional pain having to do with a love relationship, or a pain of limitation or restriction. The only reason that pain is there is because life has a way of alerting you to the fact that it's time to move to a new level of consciousness where you can accept more and be fulfilled. Remember the food that you seek is immediately available. Whether it be Love, Harmony, Prosperity or Creative Self Expression, Divine Mind stands by ready to respond to your hunger pain, waiting for you to claim your good.

So, when you feel stress or pain, don't condemn it and don't run away from it. Dare to give thanks for it. It's a sign that you are alive! Listen to your pain and let it show you how to go in the direction of your fulfillment. Forgive yourself for momentary negative feelings and use them constructively. Let them lead you to the Source of Supply and they will never again have dominion over you.

Chapter 11

The Laws Of Prosperity

We must recognize that we live in an abundant Universe. We can see evidence of it everywhere. Just drive along the Wilshire District in Los Angeles, cruise Beverly Hills or any wealthy district in any city and you will realize the tremendous amounts of money that exist in this Universe. You have every right to experience this wealth too. God did not decide that you were going to be limited.

People who are truly prosperous are into the circulation of life. They know how to accept their good and they instinctively give of themselves spontaneously to their world. They are vital, active, creative and fun to be around. They have learned the great value of contributing to their world and they have learned just how to utilize their talents and abilities to bring happiness to others. Their reward in the form of prosperity is automatic.

Whether they realize it or not they are obeying five fundamental laws that make their success possible — The Law of Receiving, the Law of Assimilation, The Law of Elimination, The Law of Giving and the Law of Multiplication.

The proper use of these natural laws will determine the degree of prosperity you will experience. These Laws are as exacting as the Law of Gravity. There's only one way to use the Law of Gravity and that is to work *with* it. You can't fight it. Learn how to work with these Laws of Prosperity and you will see how they will work for you.

Chapter 12

The Law Of Receiving
Or
Learning To Accept

The first law is The Law of Receiving. You can't circulate what isn't there. Learning to receive can be a very important beginning to your new level of prosperity. Look at the importance that breathing plays in keeping you alive. When you breathe in, you deliver life-giving oxygen to your blood stream. In order for that to happen you must first inhale the oxygen from the air around you. Receiving oxygen is the starting point of sustaining life. It activates all of the other laws that ensure a healthy existence. We must learn the art of receiving in order to qualify for the prosperous life.

Receiving what from whom? Learn to receive in two ways: First, improve your ability to receive graciously from others. To paraphrase Kahlil Gibran, do not offend the giver by trying to give something in return. There is a tendency for us to feel that all gifts carry with them a subtle message that says, "Now you're obligated to me." In truth, the only obligation you really have is to develop your sense of self worth and the courage it takes to permit the fullness of life to move into your experience in ever greater degrees so that you can enjoy the gifts.

If you believe that you are a worthy person, then prove it by accepting your good from others happily. If you receive in joy you give added joy to the giver.

It is also vitally important to increase your capacity for accepting friendship and love from others. How often we sabotage a friendship or a promising love relationship by consciously turning away, not responding, not showing our appreciation, because deep down we don't feel *worthy*. Oftentimes a deep-seated fear of unworthiness makes us feel that we don't dare let people get too close to us because if they did, they might discover what we are "really" like.

Take your rightful place in the Universe by realizing that since we are all created equal in the eyes of God, we all have an equal right to experience friendship and love. You were made to receive love and the *only* thing that can prevent you from experiencing it is a false sense of unworthiness. You are here, you exist and therefore you belong in a world of loving relationships.

There's another kind of receiving that you must give attention to. This will take a little practice, but it will be time well spent. In addition to learning how to receive from the world, we need to learn how to effectively receive from the Divine Presence Within — the Gift of Spirit.

The ultimate in self worth is accepting who you really are, an expression of Life, and that Life wants to live through you to Its fullest! You exist because of a Divine Urge. The Spirit that is the Father of all Life wanted to express in a unique and particular way and chose to manifest as you. You are an important part of the unfoldment of a Divine Idea. Once I saw a sign that said, "God didn't make no junk!" That means you!

This beautiful idea that you are was created by a Divine act of Love and that Love has never left you. It is still operating in you, imparting its perfect nature of wholeness, harmony, abundance and love into your being, BUT ONLY TO THE DEGREE THAT YOU LET IT! It is what Jesus meant when he said, "It's the Father's good pleasure to give you the Kingdom."

Abundance flows into the lives of people who have a high degree of self worth. If you feel loaded down with low self esteem, if you have burdened yourself with all sorts of imagined reasons why you don't "measure up," then it's time for you to change your belief.

Remember, when you are in an attitude of "PLOMitis" (P.L.O.M. stands for Poor Li'l Ol' Me), you are not open to the idea of receiving your good. You have closed the door to the gifts of Life. You are effectively blocking the flow of the good life into your experience.

Receiving from Spirit means that you actively accept the idea that "I am a worthy, receptive channel for the gift of Life to express ... I am that expression right now ... I am a living, purposeful channel ... I am the means by which God expresses a unique and wonderful idea through me ... I release and let go of everything that is unlike the Divine Idea that I am."

Practice daily receiving that Love until you fully realize that you do deserve to inherit the "Kingdom" right here and right now, "on earth as it already is in Heaven."

Chapter 13

The Law of Assimilation
Or
Once You Accept, It's Automatic

The maintenance of a healthy body is due to the perfect Law of Assimilation, the ability to take in all of the necessary nutrients and translate them into everything that is required for the body to function in its natural healthy manner.

The Law of Assimilation is automatic. It responds to our ability to receive. Ernest Holmes said, "You mustn't get too caught up on the sophistication of our inventions because man is never going to outdo God." To the Atheists who believe there is no God, he said, "I'd like to see you take a tomato sandwhich and turn it into fingernails and bone and skin. When you can do that maybe then I'll believe as you do, and I'll be an Atheist too."

This marvelous process of assimilation that translates into a healthy body is the same process that will bring prosperity into your experience as a healthy expression of life. You will experience it as effortlessly as your physical body automatically converts every useful ingredient into fingernails, bone and skin.

When you do your part by learning how to receive, the Law

of Assimilation does the rest. The Law of Mind knows exactly what to do with your increased ability to accept your good. It gives you a life of freedom through the abundant life.

Chapter 14

The Law Of Elimination
Or
Making Room For The New

An indication that you are ready to receive new prosperity into your life is when you learn how to make room for the new. We all have areas in our living experience that need more order. Check out those areas in your living quarters or at work where there is congestion. Think about those closets or drawers that need organizing. Think about your room. What about the storeroom or your garage?

There are two attitudes that contribute to a lack of order. One is that we do not let go of what needs to be released because "Someday we might be able to use it," (even though it's nothing more than a matchbook with one match left in it or a can of paint that dried out five years ago, still sitting in the garage). The other attitude has to do with an inability to deal appropriately with what we now have in a constructive manner. We tend to put things aside. We think, "I'll deal with it later," until it finally is buried, out of sight, forgotten and rendered useless. Neither of these attitudes is conducive to prosperous living.

In order to be open to the gifts that exist for you in this

abundant Universe, you must establish a consciousness of order so that you can make room for the new. If you don't create the void, the good that you seek has nowhere to land. When you make room for the new you may become a little frightened, a little empty. Keep remembering your good is at hand. Activate your desire. Remember, hunger is a necessary step toward fulfillment. God does not want you to be poor or restricted in any way. God doesn't want you to merely exist or just barely make it. It is the Divine Nature to provide more than enough. The Universe is extravagant. There are more apples on the tree than are ever needed, enough to plant new trees, enough to feed the birds, you and me, other animals and even then, some just lie on the ground and are never used. MORE THAN ENOUGH. THAT'S FOR YOU!

As long as you keep your life congested and full of disorganized "stuff," you are not open to letting the new move into your life. Sometimes it takes courage to release the old because some of us have a "pack rat" consciousness. When we hold on to that old bolt or screw, or whatever it is that we think we might use some day, (provided it's catalogued and in a very orderly place), what we are really saying is, "When I need it I will not have the money to go out and get it." The Law of Mind says, "Amen, brother or sister . . . so be it!"

Pick a spot in your home that is messy and promise yourself that you are going to make room for the new by releasing whatever is no longer useful to you. Throw it away, whatever it is that is of no use to anyone. When you do, *know* that you are getting ready to receive the new. While you're at it, let the physical act of releasing trigger you into letting go of the thoughts of restriction and unworthiness that up to now have been interfering with your prosperous potential. In other words, "clean up your act both physically and mentally!"

Whatever you find that may be useful to someone else, either give it away or sell it. By placing it into circulation you are establishing, for yourself, a readiness to receive even more through the Law of Multiplication, which will be explained later. If your church has a Thrift Shop, make use of it. If not, there are many organizations in your community that will joyfully receive good usable items. You will be amazed at the things that you have that other people could be using right now. Or, if you wish, hold a yard or garage sale and demonstrate some of that prosperity you've been looking for.

The next step is probably the greatest fun of all. When you go through all that "stuff" you will find things that you forgot you had. You'll discover treasures that used to be important to you, things perhaps of a sentimental value. Don't return them to obscurity. Bring them out into the open where you can enjoy them — old pictures, souvenirs of places visited long ago, whatever had meaning to you at one time that still gives you a good feeling when you see it. This can be exciting. Don't worry about how these things look to others, that doesn't matter. It's how they make you feel that counts. Bring them out and make them a part of your living environment where you can enjoy them every day and perhaps "show them off" to your friends. I know many people who have responded to this idea who have magnificent displays of old photographs on their walls.

When I was a young boy I lived on a farm with my grandparents. We had a door bell on the kitchen door, the kind that went "CLANG . . . CLANG . . . CLANG" when you turned the crank. It was so loud, you could hear it way out in the barn. It was made back in the 1800's so, of course, it was an antique. As a child that didn't impress me. I just enjoyed the wonderful noise it made and played with it often. Years later, when my grandfather sold the farm, he removed the door bell and stored it away without my knowledge. Shortly before he passed on, while I was visiting him one day, he disappeared into his closet and emerged with the door bell in his hand. He said, "Here's something you might like to have." It had been thirty years since I had seen it. I never dreamed I would see it again. It was one of the most thoughtful and beautiful gifts I have ever received.

That old door bell now has a special place on my fireplace mantel, right out front where I can share it with everyone. When I turn the crank for my friends to hear it go "CLANG... CLANG... CLANG," a rush of memories comes over me — my grandfather and grandmother and many happy days spent on the farm, the playground of my boyhood — memories that I will continue to enjoy and share with others for many years to come.

Bring those treasures out and use them. If you're not using them you're not demonstrating your abundance. You're not utilizing all that you now have and are likely missing some wonderful experiences.

Open the door to the new by letting go of all you cannot actively use and enjoy. Send it on its way with the awareness that your courage to release the old enables you to welcome the new. By releasing old thoughts and things, you allow the flow of abundant life to find a natural outlet through your own experience, and that's called personal fulfillment.

Chapter
15

The Law Of Giving
Or
Now That You Have It, Share It

The next step is just as important as all of those leading up to it. It is the ultimate demonstration of our belief in these Laws. That is, giving the very best that is in you to your world. The act of giving goes far beyond freely releasing money and things. It means giving the beautiful gift of who you are as a person. This is love of the highest order expressing through you.

The truly abundant and happy people in this world are those who have discovered the gift within themselves that needs to be given, and who actively share it with others. I think it's tragic that so many people today are living only half a life because they are doing what they think they "should" do and have denied the song within them that wants desperately to be sung. There is no greater gift you can give yourself than to promise, "I will give that which is uniquely mine to give." Your happiness is dependent upon your discovering your own contribution to your world.

Don't get upset about not knowing what your contribution is now, or will be. You get enough of "What do you want to do when you grow up?", "What are you going to major in when you go to college?" Seventy-five percent of all college students change their major by their senior year. Why? Because it's almost impossible to know what you want to do until you've had a chance to experience more of what life has to offer. In fact, I'm fifty-one years old and I *still* don't know what I want to be when I grow up!

I really believe that you don't have to know. There is that within you that does know and you have the ability to get in touch with it on a daily basis. What good is it going to do if you worry about what you're going to be doing ten years from now?

Maybe you don't think you are talented. Perhaps you are not even aware of what your true interests are. But Infinite Mind has already taken care of that because the Intelligence that created you must have had a wonderful purpose. Divine Mind creates for only positive reasons. The gifts that are yours to give may already be revealing themselves through that which you currently love to do, the activities that you find yourself attracted to.

Emerson said, "Man is surrounded by an infinite variety of opportunities from which each selects that which is his own. The talent is the call."

Begin by becoming more aware of what captures your interest today. When you are in a department store, what section do you usually head for first? When you are reading a newspaper, what section do you turn to first? What magazines are you attracted to? What is likely to capture your attention? What interests you now may not stay with you for the rest of your life. What's important is that right now you have interests. If you pursue them they may lead to other areas of interest that you are not even aware of. But for the present give attention to what you enjoy right now. Divine Mind is trying to tip you off.

As a child and a teenager I passed through many stages of interests. I studied radio and television. I studied writing. I even performed magic as a hobby. Without my realizing it at the time, every single one of my interests was preparing me for what I now do. Here I am writing, appearing on radio and television, and yes, I've even been known to illustrate Spiritual Principles by the use of magic.

I believe so strongly in the importance of exploring one's interests that I've tried, as much as possible, to support my own children's interests. It doesn't matter whether they will be involved in it for the rest of their lives or not. What matters is that the interest is there. It is a signal that something within them needs to be encouraged, explored and expressed. I believe that one of the most significant gifts parents can give their children is total support and validation of their natural interests. Children thus nurtured are likely to be valuable contributors to their world.

There's something deep within all of us that knows that unique gift we have to give. We need only trust that it's there and learn how to tap into it. You have it all: the talent, the imagination, the interest, the energy and the ability to accomplish it. When Life creates a gift, it also creates everything necessary for it to be expressed and enjoyed in your world. That is INTELLIGENCE in action. It would never create the gift without providing the means for its expression. There is a song within you that wants to be sung.

Chapter 16

The Law Of Multiplication
Or
Why You Receive More Than You Give

One of the most fascinating of all Spiritual Laws is the Law of Multiplication. It is an important law because it is the only means by which the Universe is able to perpetuate itself. It is also the law that ensures that whatever you place into the Universe returns to you in increased amounts. We are surrounded by Nature's examples of this great law.

Do you know what a redwood seed looks like? A shred of tobacco. It's a very tiny seed. If there had been redwood trees in the Holy Land, Jesus might have used the example of the redwood seed rather than the mustard seed to illustrate what a small amount of faith can do. One tiny redwood seed planted and properly nurtured not only produces one of the largest and strongest trees in the world, but a multitude of more seeds for the forests of the future.

The Law of Multiplication is based on the very simple principle that when you plant a seed it doesn't just produce another single seed. It grows into a plant, or a tree that bears fruit, which contains hundreds and sometimes thousands of seeds, more than is ever needed! A kernel of corn produces a stalk with several ears, each ear containing many kernels of corn. Think of the number of fields of corn that can be produced by just one kernel. It boggles the mind. All that is necessary is for the seed to be planted in appropriate soil and then reasonable nurturing for a period of time. Nature takes care of the rest.

This same law is working for you right now. Thoughts are like seeds. Whatever beliefs you have accepted about yourself and your world have multiplied into your present experience. Every feeling that you have expands and grows into your future expression of life.

When you are aware of such feelings as fear, resentment or jealousy, don't feel wrong or guilty about them. But do try to see that there is some illusion that is supporting them, usually false beliefs related to low self worth or that others are responsbile for your experience. By your willingness to examine those false concepts and by taking full responsibility for your challenges, you will begin the process of lessening your reinforcement of them. By refusing to nurture them they will no longer tend to multiply into your future experience. If you don't provide mental food for your false concepts, they will starve.

As you put this idea into practice, start making the Law of Multiplication work for you in a positive way by planting new seed ideas about you. Actively dwell on the beautiful gift to life that you really are and let yourself be an instrument of Divine Love. Remember that Life chose to express as you and It loves the expression of life that It is as you. That love is pure and unconditional because it is not based on how well you have performed or what you have done in this life up to this point. It conceives you to be absolutely worthy just because you are you.

THE LAW OF MULTIPLICATION

As you let this idea into your consciousness, you will be planting seeds of love and beauty that will return to you multiplied. That is the law!

The Law of Multiplication works in very tangible ways as well, for whatever you need more of, you must plant the equivalent seed and it will return to you multiplied.

Where would the farmer be if he reaped an abundant wheat harvest and sold or consumed the entire harvest? Obviously there would be no seeds left to plant and there would be nothing to harvest next year.

It works with money, too! The idea of planting seed money is not new, but it is still often ignored by many people. Many financially successful people have practiced this principle for years and would not dream of stopping it. They know they can't afford to. Therefore, if you wish to harvest more money, you need to plant tangible money seeds in such a way that the Law of Multiplication will work for you. Successful people have discovered that the most effective way to do this is to take a percentage of what they have already harvested and return it to the Source. The true Source, of course, is God but the source as it applies to this principle, means the individuals or the organization that is largely responsible for your Spiritual unfoldment.

First determine what is the major source of your inspiration and make that the recipient of your seeds. Start with a percentage of your income that is comfortable for you. As you begin to demonstrate the results in the form of an increased harvest, you will find that you will want to increase the percentage you give. Your desire to increase the percentage given will continue easily and effortlessly until you reach the amount that the ancients determined would ensure the maximum harvest . . . that is ten percent.

Whatever your source of inspiration may be, make a commitment to yourself — "I now plan to return a certain percentage of what I am already receiving to the Source of my inspiration." Be sure that you do this with a sense of joy and freedom, not out of duty or bargaining with the Universe.

I don't know what that source of inspiration is for you. If it's a church then let it be a church. It doesn't matter how much you give in the beginning. What matters is that you get into the habit of giving so that the Law of Multiplication will work for you. YOU are responsible for "letting" prosperity happen to you. YOU are responsible for planting the seeds that will multiply for good.

Chapter 17

So Sing Your Song

You are a special person in this Universe and you have something very special to give. You have some tools now and it's up to you to use them. Giving the best that is in you is what living is all about. When you really stop to think about it, what point is there to living unless we LIVE the life that is ours to live? Ernest Holmes said, "It is not necessary, if we should pass on tonight, that anyone should remember that we have ever lived. All that means anything is that WHILE WE LIVE, WE LIVE..."

Living is Self expressing. It means giving that which you are, to yourself and to your world, because you are a Divine Idea that wants to express. That idea chose to express as YOU! It knows what It's doing! You are a magnificent idea in the Mind of God and that idea wants out. It wants to get out there and LIVE. It wants to experience the freedom of a prosperous life. It wants to explore the world. It wants to surround itself with beauty. It wants to create fulfillment for you in every part of your life, for in so doing, It has found an outlet for Its own desire to express Itself more fully and more completely THROUGH YOU, It's beloved creation.

You have the right to fully enjoy your world, and you shall

so long as you continue to strive towards discovering more of who and what you are. Practice letting the uniqueness of your being freely and fully express in all of its wonder and beauty. **You have the right to live in the fullness of life. You have the right to BE ALL THAT YOU ARE DESIGNED TO BE.**

*"A few can touch the magic strings
and noisy fame is proud to win them.*

*Alas, for those that never sing,
but die with all their music in them."*

***SO SING! SING YOUR SONG
FOR ALL YOU'RE WORTH!***